Earth Science

Peter Pentland and
Pennie Stoyles

CHELSEA HOUSE
PUBLISHERS

A Haights Cross Communications Company

Philadelphia

This edition first published in 2003 in the United States of America by Chelsea House Publishers, a subsidiary of Haights Cross Communications.

Chelsea House Publishers
1974 Sproul Road, Suite 400
Broomall, PA 19008-0914

The Chelsea House world wide web address is www.chelseahouse.com

Library of Congress Cataloging-in-Publication Data

Pentland, Peter.
    Earth science / by Peter Pentland and Pennie Stoyles.
    v. cm. — (Science and scientists)

    Includes index.
    Contents: Have you ever wondered ...? — How was the earth formed and what is it made of? — Is the earth's crust all in one piece? — What is an earthquake? — How can you measure an earthquake? — Tsunamis: what are they? — What is a volcano? — How are volcanoes formed? — Meet a volcanologist — What is there between here and space? — Weather — Why does it rain, hail and snow? — What are lightning and thunder? — Wild winds — Earth science timeline.
    ISBN 0-7910-7012-3
    1. Earth sciences—Juvenile literature. [1. Earth sciences.] I. Stoyles, Pennie. II. Title.
    QE29 .P46 2003
    550—dc21

                                                        2002001283

First published in 2002 by
MACMILLAN EDUCATION AUSTRALIA PTY LTD
627 Chapel Street, South Yarra, Australia, 3141

Copyright © Peter Pentland and Pennie Stoyles 2002

Copyright in photographs © individual photographers as credited

Edited by Sally Woollett
Text design by Nina Sanadze
Cover design by Nina Sanadze
Illustrations by Pat Kermode, Purple Rabbit Productions

Printed in China

Acknowledgements
Cover: Mount Etna volcano erupting, courtesy of Otto Hahn/Peter Arnold/Auscape.

AAP/AP Photo/Itsuo Inouye, p. 10; Jean-Paul Ferrero/Auscape, pp. 24–25; Otto Hahn/Peter Arnold/Auscape, pp. 16–17; Kevin Hamdorf/Auscape, p. 18 (right); P. Lorne/Explorer/Auscape, p. 4 (left); Kevin Schafer/Peter Arnold/Auscape, pp. 5 (top right), 8–9; Image obtained by Japan's Geostationary Meteorological Satellite and processed by the Australian Bureau of Meteorology, pp. 5 (bottom right), 29 (top); Australian Picture Library, p. 29 (bottom); Australian Picture Library/Corbis, p. 12; Bureau of Meteorology, p. 22; Dr Ray Cas, p. 19; Coo-ee Historical Picture Library, p. 14; Coo-ee Picture Library, pp. 5 (left), 9 (right), 23, 26–27; Getty Images/Photodisc, pp. 4 (right), 18 (left), 28; NASA, p. 21; US Navy/NOAA, p. 15.

Contents

Glossary words

When a word is printed in bold you can look up its meaning in the Glossary on page 31.

Science terms

When a word appears like this **dissolved** 🔍 you can find out more about it in the science term box located nearby.

Have you ever wondered...

...why volcanoes erupt?

...what causes storms?

...why some natural disasters only seem to happen in some parts of the world?

...what it would be like to travel to the center of Earth?

Did you know that all the answers have something to do with science?

What is earth science?

Earth science is the study of Earth and its atmosphere. Earth science helps people to understand how and why natural disasters and other weather events happen. Natural disasters affect millions of people every year. They are called natural because the forces of nature cause them. They are called disasters if they have a bad effect on people or on the natural environment. It is a disaster if many people are killed or injured. It is a disaster if houses and buildings are destroyed. It is a disaster if communities no longer have important things such as fresh food and water, shelter, medical supplies and power.

Scientists

No one has ever gone to the center of Earth. In fact, the deepest hole ever drilled was only about 9 miles (15 kilometers) deep. Earth scientists have come up with a picture of what Earth must be like inside by studying volcanoes, earthquakes and rock formations. They have found out about things that happen in our atmosphere by using weather balloons and other instruments.

What we know about Earth and its atmosphere is the result of hundreds of years of work.

There are many types of scientists and they all have different jobs to do.

⊙ Meteorologists study and predict the weather.

⊙ Seismologists find out about Earth and why earthquakes happen.

⊙ Volcanologists find out about volcanoes.

In this book you will:

⊙ find out about Earth's formation and structure

⊙ learn about earthquakes, tsunamis and volcanoes

⊙ meet someone who knows all about volcanoes

⊙ learn all about the atmosphere and the causes of the weather

⊙ find out what causes thunder and lightning.

▲ Satellite image of the San Andreas Fault Line.

▲ Satellite image of a tropical storm.

How was Earth formed and what is it made of?

Have you ever wondered how Earth was formed? Where did all the stuff that formed Earth come from? What is it like inside Earth? If people have never traveled to the center of Earth, how do they know what is there?

How was Earth formed?

Earth was formed about 4.6 billion years ago. Scientists believe that a star exploded. This threw out a huge cloud of dust. The dust cloud was made up of lots of different kinds of materials, from very light gases to very heavy metals.

The **force** of **gravity** pulled on the cloud of gas and it began to get smaller. The Sun formed in the center of the cloud. The rest of the cloud became the planets, their moons, the **asteroids** and the **comets**.

Earth was one of the planets that formed from the cloud of gas and dust. It first formed into a huge ball of matter that was basically the same all the way through.

As the ball became smaller because of the force of gravity, it got hotter and melted. Heavy materials like iron and nickel collected at the center of the ball. The ball then cooled and the outside formed a solid crust.

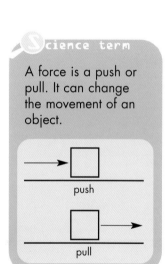

Science term

A force is a push or pull. It can change the movement of an object.

push

pull

The formation of the solar system and Earth is thought to have been caused by a huge explosion.

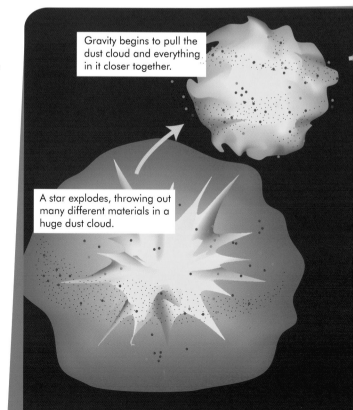

Gravity begins to pull the dust cloud and everything in it closer together.

A star explodes, throwing out many different materials in a huge dust cloud.

Inside Earth

Earth is shaped like a slightly flattened ball. It is flattened at the north and south **poles**. It is made up of a number of layers.

The crust

The outside layer is called the crust. It is between 25 and 44 miles (40 and 70 kilometers) thick and is made up of solid rock. The outside of the crust is the surface of Earth. Further down through the crust the temperature rises to about 700 degrees Fahrenheit (about 375 degrees Celsius).

The mantle

The next layer is called the mantle. It is about 1,800 miles (2,900 kilometers) thick. In the top part of the mantle, the rocks tend to melt and can even flow. The rocks of the rest of the mantle are more like modeling clay—they can still move, but only very slowly. The temperature where the mantle and the outer core meet is about 6,330 degrees Fahrenheit (3,500 degrees Celsius).

The core

Within the mantle is the core of Earth. It consists of an inner and outer core. It is made up mainly of iron and nickel. The outer core is made of melted rock. The inner core is hotter than the outer core, but very high pressure makes it solid. The temperature at the center of Earth is extremely hot—about 8,100 degrees Fahrenheit (4,500 degrees Celsius).

Inside information

• The mantle makes up 82 percent of Earth's volume.

• The inner core of Earth is bigger than the Moon.

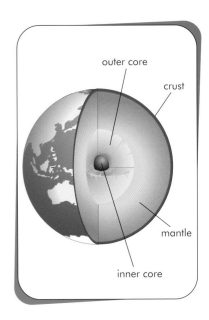

Earth is made up of a crust, a mantle and a core.

How do scientists know what is inside Earth?

Scientists have built up a model of the structure of Earth by studying the ways shock waves from earthquakes travel through the inside of Earth.

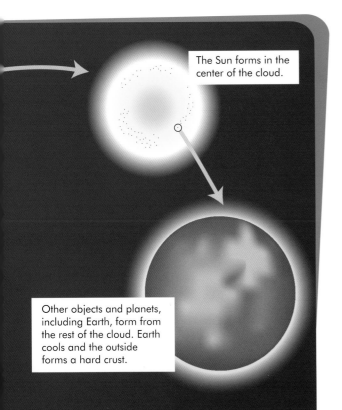

The Sun forms in the center of the cloud.

Other objects and planets, including Earth, form from the rest of the cloud. Earth cools and the outside forms a hard crust.

The moving crust

If all the water from the oceans disappeared, you could see that the crust of Earth is actually made up of many pieces. The pieces of Earth are called **tectonic** plates. They are slowly sliding around on top of the mantle.

The moving plates can push together, pull apart or slide past each other. When the plates push together, one plate slides underneath the other. This forms a deep ocean trench where the plates meet. This process also pushes the second plate up and forms mountains. And it causes earthquakes and volcanoes.

When the plates pull apart, the mantle below the crust can melt, because pressure is released, and come to the surface. This forms ridges on the floor of the ocean.

When the plates slide past each other they rub together and can cause earthquakes.

Volcanoes can occur when one plate is forced beneath another, or when plates pull apart.

Science term

Tectonics is the study of the way that Earth has formed its structure.

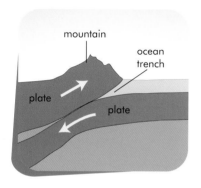

One plate sliding under another can cause earthquakes and volcanoes.

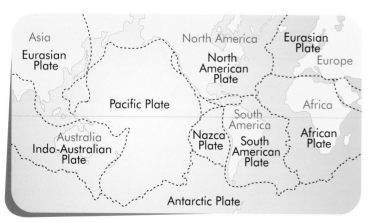

Earth's continents sit on top of the tectonic plates. The names of the larger plates are shown here.

Seismologists

Seismologists are scientists who study earthquakes. They have discovered why earthquakes happen and the regions where earthquakes are most likely to happen. Their work helps to make regions where earthquakes happen safer to live in. One thing that seismologists have discovered is the reason why the plates drift.

Why the plates are moving

The heat at the core of Earth is caused by **radioactivity**. The hot core makes the rock of the mantle move around. The material at the bottom of the mantle gets hot. It rises to the top where it is pushed along by more rising rock. It then cools and sinks back down to the bottom again. One complete cycle takes millions of years. As the mantle moves under the crust, it pushes the plates along.

The Himalayan mountain range has been formed by two plates pushing together.

Earthquakes sometimes happen when one plate slides past another along the San Andreas Fault line in California.

What is an earthquake?

Science fact

Damage details

- In 1966 an earthquake in Tashkent, Russia, lasted for 38 days.

- An earthquake in Prince William Sound, Alaska, carried a six-story building 10 feet (3 meters) sideways without damaging it.

- In January 1994, an earthquake in Los Angeles killed 57 people and caused more than $20 billion dollars worth of damage.

Have you ever experienced an earthquake? What causes earthquakes? Why do some areas have more earthquakes than others?

An earthquake is a violent shaking or trembling of Earth's surface. When an earthquake happens it can:

⊙ shake buildings apart

⊙ cause the ground to split

⊙ lift one part of the crust above another

⊙ cause **landslides**

⊙ break water, sewage and gas pipes

⊙ break electricity and telephone cables.

An earthquake in Nishinomiya, Japan, in 1995 warped these railway lines.

Earthquake science

Earth's crust is made up of plates that are slowly moving. When the plates push together or slide past one another they grip onto each other and there is a buildup of pressure. The rock plates bend and store **energy** 🔍.

The rock in the plates eventually breaks. The energy that was stored in the rocks is released and travels through the crust in shock waves, like ripples moving across the surface of a pond. These waves cause the crust to **vibrate**. When this happens an earthquake is occurring.

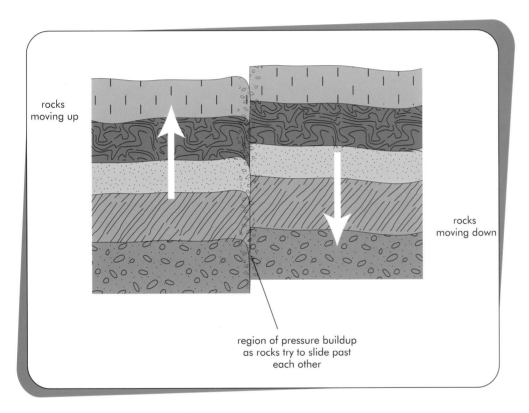

rocks moving up

rocks moving down

region of pressure buildup as rocks try to slide past each other

Before an earthquake there is a buildup of pressure.

The deepest earthquakes happen when one plate is pushed under another plate. Shallow earthquakes happen when the plates slide past each other. Shallow earthquakes are sometimes very strong. The San Andreas Fault on the western coast of the North American continent is a good example of plates sliding past each other.

Any buildup of pressure in the rock of the crust can cause an earthquake. Such an increase in pressure can be caused by volcanic eruptions, other earthquakes or underground nuclear explosions.

How can you measure an earthquake?

How do scientists measure the strength of an earthquake? What is the Richter scale? What is the epicenter of an earthquake? How do scientists find the exact position of an earthquake?

Detecting earthquakes

Scientists detect earthquakes using instruments called seismographs. These instruments are set in the ground and measure the **seismic** waves. A seismograph is a heavy mass hanging in springs in a frame. The frame is connected to the rock of Earth's crust. The mass controls a set of pens that make lines on a chart. The chart is attached to a slowly turning drum mounted on the frame. When an earthquake shakes the ground, the drum shakes too but the heavy mass stays still. This produces a set of wavy lines on the seismograph. The marked chart is called a seismogram.

Seismic means 'of earthquakes'. It comes from the Greek word *seio* meaning 'to shake'.

Finding where the earthquake occurred

Scientists can locate where an earthquake occurred by looking at the data from seismograms at three or more different positions on the surface of Earth. They note the time when the shock waves reached each seismograph. They know how fast shock waves travel through the crust so they are then able to calculate how far the earthquake was from each seismograph and then where exactly the earthquake occurred.

The epicenter

The place on the surface of Earth that is exactly above the part of the crust where the earthquake occurred is called the epicenter of the earthquake.

This seismograph shows normal movement of Earth. The pattern made by the pen is regular.

Measuring strength

Once the scientists know where the earthquake occurred, they can then work out how strong it was.

The strength of an earthquake is measured using the Richter scale. This gives the strength of the earthquake as a whole number and a decimal place. It is a special scale because if one earthquake is a whole number bigger than another on the Richter scale, it is really ten times more powerful.

The Richter scale for different earthquakes

Richter scale   What usually happens on Earth

Richter scale	What usually happens on Earth
0	This can only be detected using seismographs
1	Only a few people notice these
2	Hanging light shades sway noticeably
3	Hanging light shades sway violently
4	Small objects such as vases fall over
5	Stone structures fall apart
6	Landslides occur
7	Buildings collapse

Tsunamis: what are they?

Do you know what a tsunami is? What makes a tsunami so destructive? In what ways does a tsunami cause damage?

Tsunami is a Japanese word that means 'harbor wave'. A tsunami is a giant set of waves that crashes onto a coast. The waves often destroy vegetation and communities as huge volumes of water flow inland.

Tsunamis do not start out as big waves. The waves get bigger as they approach land because the water there is shallower than in the middle of the ocean. The waves move more slowly, bunch up and get even higher. When the waves reach the shore the water keeps moving inland until it has lost all of its energy.

When a tsunami reaches a coast, it can destroy boats and harbor buildings. It strips sand from beaches that may have taken years to build up. When the water comes onto the shore it can knock over trees and buildings and strip off vegetation. The water then carries **debris** that causes more damage. Electricity and telephone lines are cut. Water supplies are polluted with salt water, mud, debris and the bodies of dead animals. Diseases can develop quickly.

This Japanese woodblock print of a tsunami is called *The Great Wave of Kanazawa*.

This parking meter was knocked flat by the 1960 tsunami that hit Hawaii.

Tsunami science

Tsunamis can result from earthquakes that occur under the oceans. The ocean floor may be suddenly lifted or dropped. This affects the water above that area and produces a series of high waves that are very long. The waves spread out in all directions from the epicenter of the earthquake. Other events that cause tsunamis are meteor strikes, landslides and underwater volcanic eruptions.

Scientists who study tsunamis have found that a tsunami's size depends on:

⊙ the size of the earthquake that caused the tsunami. This determines how much energy is passed into the ocean

⊙ the distance of the shore from the epicenter. This is important because the farther the waves travel the more spread out their energy is and the waves get smaller. Think of throwing a rock into the middle of a pond. As the waves move away from where the splash occurred, the size of the waves gets smaller because the energy of the wave is spread out over a much bigger circle

⊙ the time of arrival of the tsunami at the coast. This is important because the maximum damage will be done if the tsunami arrives at high tide.

Tsunamis can be caused by other natural events.

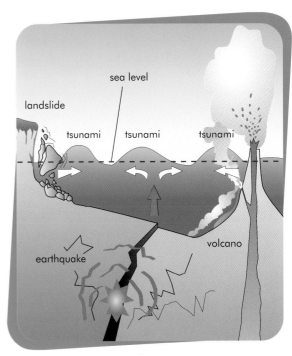

What is a volcano?

A volcano is a place on the surface of Earth where melted rock from beneath the crust forces its way to the surface. When the melted rock is beneath the surface it is called magma; when it passes out onto the surface it is called lava.

What makes the rock melt?

The crust and mantle are basically solid rock. Deeper in Earth the temperature and pressure increase. If the temperature of the rock increases and the pressure decreases for some reason, the rock will melt. The presence of water in the rock will also help to melt the rock.

How do people find out about volcanoes?

Scientists who study volcanoes are called volcanologists. Volcanologists study how volcanoes are made and what comes out of them. They try to predict when and where volcanoes will erupt and what will happen if an eruption occurs.

This volcano is called Mount Etna. It is in southern Italy.

Could a volcano erupt where you live?

Have you ever wondered if a volcano could erupt under your house? Why do volcanoes only seem to happen in certain parts of the world and not in others?

Volcanoes generally occur at points where the plates that make up the surface of Earth pull apart.

Volcanoes can also occur where plates collide and one plate slides under the other. The rocks in the plate that is sinking are absorbed into the mantle. These rocks will contain water and melt easily.

The melted rock is not as dense as the surrounding rock and rises to the surface, forcing its way through weak patches in the crust.

The sloping shape of the volcano is called the cone. The cone is made up of alternate layers of ash and solid lava. The tube in the center of the volcano is called a vent or a conduit.

Two plates pull apart. This releases the pressure on the mantle. The rock of the mantle melts and magma is formed. The magma flows to the surface of the crust.

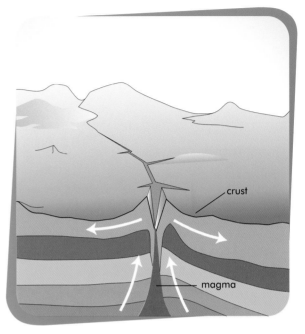

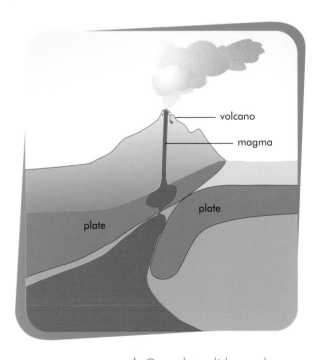

▲ One plate slides under another. This can cause rock to melt and result in a volcano.

How are volcanoes formed?

Every volcano has a different shape. Some are steep cones, others are flat and look a bit like shields. Why do volcanoes have different shapes? To understand this you need to know a bit about what comes out of a volcano and how it comes out.

What comes out of a volcano?

When the melted rock (magma) comes out of a volcano it can flow down the side of the volcano as lava. Some lavas are thin and runny and they flow quickly. Other lavas are thick like honey and flow very slowly.

Magma has a lot of gas in it. When the pressure is released from the magma during an eruption the gas forms bubbles. This is like taking the lid off a bottle of soft drink.

Many volcanoes also produce volcanic ash. The ash is not the same as wood ash that you get after a fire. It might be fine rock dust that can be formed when the rock of the countryside is blown apart as the volcano first erupts. Or it can be made from smashed-up pieces of magma.

Types of volcanoes

Some volcanoes have steep-sided cones formed by alternate layers of thick, slow-moving lava and ash. Others are shield-shaped. These are formed by fast-flowing, runny lava.

This shield volcano is in Hawaii.

This steep volcano is in the Philippines.

Meet a volcanologist

Have you ever asked yourself what it would be like to work as an Earth scientist? What sorts of jobs are there? How is it possible to get a job? What do you have to study in high school and at college?

Meet Ray Cas

Ray Cas has the answers to these questions. He is a volcanologist who works at a university's department of earth sciences. He teaches about and does research on volcanoes.

Ray grew up and went to school in Sydney, Australia. He became interested in science in high school, where he studied mathematics and science. He also enjoyed English, especially literature and writing.

Ray went to university wanting to become an **industrial chemist**. He soon discovered the fascinating world of geology. He found out about the restless Earth, earthquakes, the huge scale of geological time, the **evolution** of life and, of course, volcanoes.

After finishing a Bachelor of Science degree, Ray did further study on volcanoes and finally graduated as a doctor of science.

Ray Cas (right) and a group of other researchers visited the Tuzgle volcano in the Andes, South America.

Ray thinks he has one of the best jobs in the world. He loves teaching new students about geology, and especially about volcanoes. He loves doing research and helping students develop a wide range of skills.

Ray also works with the mining industry and travels all over the world to work on volcanoes and ancient volcanic rocks in such places as South America, the Mediterranean, the Canary Islands, Hawaii and Greenland.

Ray says that volcanology is great fun. He thinks it is one of the most interesting and exciting subject areas to study. Ray also believes choosing a subject area that you find interesting and exciting is more than half the secret to successfully completing a college degree.

What is there between here and space?

What would it be like to travel up through our atmosphere all the way into space? Why does it get colder as you go higher? Why do mountain climbers on Mount Everest need to carry their own supply of oxygen? What is the atmosphere?

The atmosphere is a thin layer of gases that surrounds Earth. Three-quarters of the mass of the atmosphere is trapped in a blanket at the surface that is only 9 miles (15 kilometers) thick.

The gases of the atmosphere are held to Earth by the force of gravity. The Moon has no atmosphere because it does not have a strong enough force of gravity to stop the air escaping into space.

Layers of the atmosphere

Four different layers make up Earth's atmosphere.

The troposphere

The troposphere is the layer closest to Earth. It is about 9 miles (15 kilometers) thick over the **equator**, but only about 5 miles (8 kilometers) thick over the poles. It bulges out over the equator because Earth is spinning on its axis. If Earth did not spin on its axis the troposphere would be the same thickness all over.

The temperature of the air in the troposphere drops by about 13 degrees Fahrenheit (7 degrees Celsius) for about every half a mile (one kilometer) you move away from Earth.

Most of the clouds form in the troposphere. Nearly all the weather experienced on the surface of Earth begins in the troposphere. It is driven by the energy of the Sun.

Earth's atmosphere has four layers.

Miles above sea level
300

exosphere

space shuttle

ionosphere

thunder cloud

very high clouds

weather balloon

jet airliner

50

ozone layer

10

stratosphere

troposphere

Earth

An aurora is caused by charged particles from the Sun hitting gas particles in the ionosphere.

The stratosphere

The stratosphere is the layer above the troposphere. It extends from the top of the troposphere to about 50 miles (80 kilometers) above sea level.

The stratosphere contains a gas called ozone. Ozone particles are made of oxygen **atoms**. Ozone is formed by electrical discharges such as lightning. The ozone in the stratosphere protects Earth from harmful **ultraviolet rays** from the Sun.

The ionosphere

The ionosphere is the layer above the stratosphere. It extends from the top of the stratosphere to about 313 miles (500 kilometers) above sea level. It is very thin and is made up of particles that have been given an electrical charge by the radiation from the Sun. The International Space Station and many other satellites orbit Earth in the upper reaches of the ionosphere.

The exosphere

The exosphere lies beyond the ionosphere. It is extremely thin and gradually disappears.

Weather

Rain, hail or shine, the weather is always there. Have you ever wondered why sometimes the weather is fine and sunny and other days are rainy or stormy? Why does the weather change? What causes the winds?

Meteorologists are scientists who study the atmosphere and the way it behaves. They are interested in:

- why winds happen
- why clouds form
- what makes rain, hail, snow and other forms of precipitation
- what happens in different types of storms.

Some meteorologists predict what the weather will be like. Their predictions are very important to people such as pilots, sailors, farmers and firefighters.

Meteorologists use special instruments such as weather balloons to predict all kinds of weather events.

What causes the weather?

The Sun causes all of our weather. It heats up the surface of Earth unevenly. Land gets hotter than water. The part of Earth directly below the Sun gets hottest. The polar areas get coldest.

Famous scientist

Admiral Fitzroy

Modern weather forecasting became possible with the invention of the electric telegraph in 1844. This allowed weather instrument readings to be collected quickly from far-flung places.

The British Meteorological Office was opened in 1854. Its first director was Admiral Fitzroy. He issued the first daily weather report in 1860. Fitzroy did not have much reliable information to work with, but he did come up with a basically correct theory to explain why regions of low pressure occur. Fitzroy died in 1865 and his theory was ignored until 1912. His theory is still considered to be correct today.

Under pressure

You live at the bottom of an ocean of air. The weight of all the air above you pushes against you. As you go higher the **air pressure** gets smaller.

The air pressure is constantly changing on the surface of Earth. Some areas have high pressure and others have low pressure.

Science term

Air pressure is a measure of how much push the air gives to an area.

Moving air

On the surface of Earth, the air naturally flows from high-pressure areas to low-pressure areas. Trees, hills, cities and mountains can slow the flow of air on land. Air moving across oceans is able to move very quickly, because there is nothing slowing it down.

The speed of the moving air across Earth's surface depends on how far apart the high-pressure and low-pressure zones are and the difference in pressure. Strong winds occur when there is a large difference in air pressures and the pressure zones are close together.

Waves are caused by wind moving across water.

Science fact

Air facts

• Moving air causes waves on water.

• When you sneeze, air rushes out of your mouth and nose at speeds of up to 94 miles (150 kilometers) an hour.

Why does it rain, hail and snow?

Have you ever wondered why cars look so dirty after a shower of rain? The answer to this question can be found in the clouds.

What causes clouds?

Water vapor in the air causes clouds to form. Warm air can hold a lot of water vapor. The hot air can rise by itself. It can also be lifted up by a mass of cold air sliding in underneath it, or it can be forced to rise by mountains. As the hot, water-filled air rises, it gets colder. It can no longer hold as much water vapor. Water droplets form around dust particles in the air and a cloud forms. The droplets are so small that they float in the air.

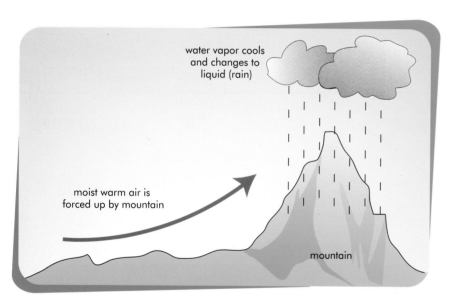

water vapor cools and changes to liquid (rain)

moist warm air is forced up by mountain

mountain

▲ Clouds are formed when warm, moist air is forced to rise by a mass of cold air or by mountains.

What causes rain?

The droplets inside a cloud bump into each other and join together. They gradually get bigger and bigger until they are so heavy that they start to fall. As they fall they join with more droplets and finally become raindrops.

24

What causes hail?

A hailstone is a frozen ball of water that falls from a cloud. Some clouds reach very high into the air. Inside these clouds there are powerful upward streams of air. Droplets of water in these streams get colder and freeze. They get bigger as more moisture freezes on their surfaces. These balls of ice eventually fall. Some melt and change back to water vapor again inside the cloud. Others melt and fall to the ground as raindrops. The ones that stay frozen and reach the ground are hailstones.

What causes snow?

Snow forms in a similar way to raindrops. Some clouds are so cold that water vapor turns straight into ice around the particles. The ice crystals get bigger as more vapor turns to ice on their surfaces. The crystals grow into snowflakes. When they are big enough they fall. They reach the ground as snowflakes if the air is cold enough. Otherwise they melt and become raindrops.

Whether water falls as rain, hail or snow depends on the air temperature.

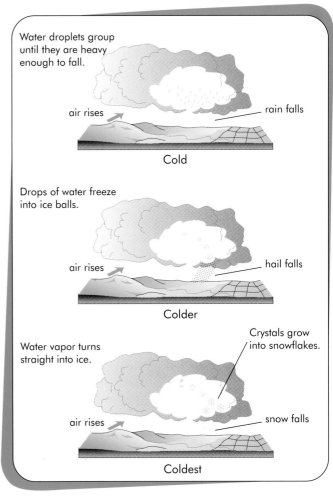

Water droplets group until they are heavy enough to fall.

air rises — rain falls

Cold

Drops of water freeze into ice balls.

air rises — hail falls

Colder

Crystals grow into snowflakes.

Water vapor turns straight into ice.

air rises — snow falls

Coldest

Can you see the blue and green covers on the roofs of these houses? The roofs were badly damaged after a hail storm.

Science fact

Dirty rain

Have you noticed that cars are dirty after a shower of rain? This is because when the water turns back into water vapor, it leaves behind the dust particles around which the water droplets had originally formed.

What are lightning and thunder?

Have you ever wondered what causes lightning and thunder? What causes thunderstorms? Why does lightning strike trees and tall buildings? How can you tell how far away the lightning is?

What causes thunderstorms?

1   Thunderstorms start when clouds are formed in rising air. This can result in a cloud that is up to 6 miles (10 kilometers) thick. The bottom of the cloud is near the ground.

2   Inside the cloud, warm, moist air rushes to the top of the cloud.

3   The air cools and the water from the air forms hailstones that fall back to the bottom of the cloud.

4   The rising warm, moist air and the falling hailstones and cold air cause the bottom of the cloud to become charged with electricity.

5   Sometimes the hailstones fall to the ground, but they usually melt and result in rain.

6   Electrical charges build up at the top and bottom of the cloud and on the ground beneath the cloud. The energy of the charges moving through the air is seen as lightning and heard as thunder.

Weird science!?

American park ranger Roy 'Dooms' Sullivan was struck by lightning seven times between 1942 and 1977 and survived each time!

This lightning strike happened in Darwin, Australia. →

Making and measuring lightning and thunder

There are two types of electrical **charge** : positive and negative. When a negatively charged bottom of a cloud comes close to the ground it attracts positive charge from the ground. If there is enough charge, a spark will jump between the ground and the cloud. This flow of charge is the lightning. The air near the lightning gets very hot and explodes, making the sound of thunder. The reason that the cloud becomes negatively charged in the first place is not well understood.

You see lightning before you hear the thunder because light travels much faster than sound. The sound of thunder takes about 5 seconds to travel 1 mile (1.6 kilometers).

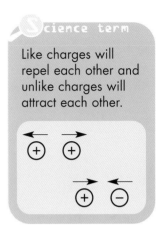

Science term

Like charges will repel each other and unlike charges will attract each other.

Try this

Next time a thunderstorm happens near you, see if you can tell how far away a lightning flash was.

1 Count how many seconds pass between seeing the lightning flash and hearing the thunder. Count slowly.

2 Divide the seconds by five and the result is the distance away in miles. Divide the seconds by three to get a rough answer in kilometers.

Have you ever wondered how tornadoes, hurricanes and tropical storms happen? Why are they so destructive?

What is a tornado?

A tornado is a rapidly spinning column of air that reaches from the bottom of a thundercloud to the ground. The force of a tornado can be strong enough to lift cars, machinery, and animals high into the air and to destroy buildings. If a tornado passes over water it picks up water and becomes a waterspout.

Tornadoes can be more than 320 feet (100 meters) across and have wind speeds of more than 190 miles (300 kilometers) an hour.

How tornadoes happen

Tornadoes start out as thunderstorms. A fast-moving body of cold air moves over an area of hot, moist air. The hot air rises rapidly through the cold air at speeds of up to 200 miles (320 kilometers) an hour. Clouds are formed in this rising air. Air rushes in to replace the rising air and it can make the rising air start to spin. This is the beginning of a tornado. The bottom of the cloud starts to twist and forms into a thin funnel. The funnel cloud then reaches down to the ground. This is when the destruction begins. Tornadoes can travel across the country at speeds more than 60 miles (100 kilometers) an hour, but many last for only a few minutes.

Air rises from the top and is replaced by more air from underneath.

spinning air

body of cold air

Warm, moist air flows in.

Hot air rises and cools. It starts to spin.

A tornado looks like this from the inside.

Where they occur

Most tornadoes happen in midwestern United States, but they can occur on most warm continents.

This is a fully formed tornado.

Satellite images can show the formation of a tropical storm.

Hurricanes and tropical storms

Hurricane and *tropical storm* are different names for intense tropical weather systems with winds faster than 78 miles (125 kilometers) an hour. The word *hurricane* comes from the Caribbean Indian word meaning 'big wind'.

How tropical storms occur

Tropical storms start over oceans. Intense regions of low pressure form as the Sun warms the water. Air starts to move from high-pressure zones into low-pressure areas. The winds have a higher speed when there is a bigger difference in pressure between the high-pressure and low-pressure areas.

As the air moves it starts to swirl around the center of the low-pressure areas. It swirls in an **counterclockwise** direction in the Northern Hemisphere and in a **clockwise** direction in the Southern Hemisphere.

Tropical storm Tracy

Hurricanes and tropical storms occur on other continents besides North America. The most famous one to hit Australia was tropical storm Tracy. Tracy destroyed the city of Darwin on Christmas Day, 1974. The maximum wind speed recorded was 136 miles (217 kilometers) an hour (before the instrument broke). Sixty-five people were killed and the damage bill was estimated to be $800 million in Australian dollars. Darwin had to be totally rebuilt after the storm.

Tropical storm Tracy did a lot of damage in Darwin, Australia, in 1974.

Earth science timeline

This timeline shows some important earth science events. See if you can imagine some of the things that might happen to Earth in the future.

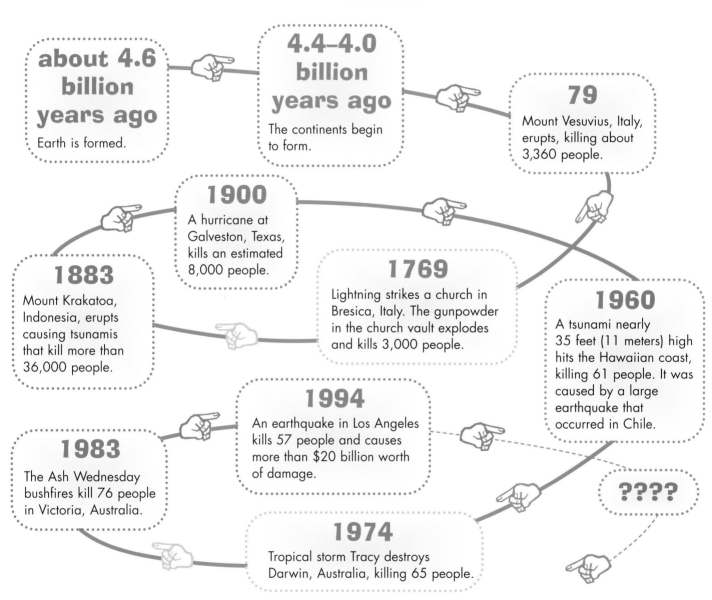

about 4.6 billion years ago
Earth is formed.

4.4–4.0 billion years ago
The continents begin to form.

79
Mount Vesuvius, Italy, erupts, killing about 3,360 people.

1900
A hurricane at Galveston, Texas, kills an estimated 8,000 people.

1883
Mount Krakatoa, Indonesia, erupts causing tsunamis that kill more than 36,000 people.

1769
Lightning strikes a church in Bresica, Italy. The gunpowder in the church vault explodes and kills 3,000 people.

1960
A tsunami nearly 35 feet (11 meters) high hits the Hawaiian coast, killing 61 people. It was caused by a large earthquake that occurred in Chile.

1994
An earthquake in Los Angeles kills 57 people and causes more than $20 billion worth of damage.

1983
The Ash Wednesday bushfires kill 76 people in Victoria, Australia.

1974
Tropical storm Tracy destroys Darwin, Australia, killing 65 people.

????

What are scientists working on now?

⊙ Scientists are trying to launch tiny rockets into tornadoes to gather information about how these weather events behave. This will allow meteorologists to make better predictions and give people more time to get to safety.

⊙ Scientists are looking at ways to accurately predict when and where earthquakes will occur.

Glossary

asteroids	large lumps of rock in orbit around the Sun
atoms	tiny particles that combine to make up all things, be they solid, liquid or gas
clockwise	in the same direction as the movement of the hands on a clock face
comets	balls of rock and ice in orbit around the Sun
counterclockwise	in the opposite direction to the movement of the hands on a clock face
debris	the wreckage left behind after a disaster
energy	the ability of an object to do work. Energy cannot be created or destroyed, but it can be changed from one form to another
equator	an imaginary circle around the surface of Earth that is midway between the north and south poles
evolution	a series of changes
force	a push or pull. It can change the movement of an object
gravity	a force that pulls all objects together
industrial chemist	a scientist that uses chemical reactions to make products for industries
landslides	movement of large masses of earth down a hill, mountain or cliff
ozone layer	the region in the stratosphere that contains particles of a gas called ozone. The ozone layer absorbs ultraviolet radiation
poles	the places on Earth's surface at the ends of Earth's axis
radioactivity	the giving off of charged particles or high-energy rays by atoms
ultraviolet rays	high-energy rays that are invisible to the human eye
vibrate	shake from side to side
water vapor	the gaseous state of water

Index